DISASTER RELIEF

Nick Hunter

www.raintreepublishers.co.uk
Visit our website to find out more information about Raintree books.

To order:
☎ Phone 0845 6044371
▤ Fax +44 (0) 1865 312263
▤ Email myorders@raintreepublishers.co.uk

Customers from outside the UK please telephone +44 1865 312262

Raintree is an imprint of **Capstone Global Library Limited**, a company incorporated in England and Wales having its registered office at 7 Pilgrim Street, London, EC4V 6LB – Registered company number: 6695582

Text © Capstone Global Library Limited 2012
First published in hardback in 2012

The moral rights of the proprietor have been asserted.

Edited by Dan Nunn, Rebecca Rissman, and Catherine Veitch
Designed by Joanne Malivoire
Picture research by Elizabeth Alexander
Originated by Capstone Global Library
Printed and bound in China by CTPS

ISBN 978 1 406 23209 7
15 14 13 12 11
10 9 8 7 6 5 4 3 2 1

British Library Cataloguing in Publication Data
Hunter, Nick.
Disaster relief. – (Heroic jobs)
363.3'48-dc22
A full catalogue record for this book is available from the British Library.

Acknowledgements
We would like to thank the following for permission to reproduce photographs: Alamy pp. 5 (© Tommy Trenchard), 6 (© Caro), 7 (© Tim Graham), 11 (© Tommy Trenchard), 15 (© Jack Sullivan); Corbis pp. 17 (© STRINGER/epa), 18 (shaheen Buneri / Demotix Images); Getty Images pp. 8 (JUAN BARRETO/AFP), 9 (POOL/AFP), 10 (Rizwan Tabassum/AFP), 12 (Alison Wright/ National Geographic), 16 (Daniel Berehulak), 25 (XINHUA/Gamma-Rapho); Photolibrary pp. 4 (Christian Kober), 20 (EPA/Guillermo Legaria), 22 (Alberto Fernandez), 23 (Matthew White), 24 (Roger Ressmeyer), 26 (Mark & Audrey Gibson), 27 (Visions LLC), 28 (Frank Polich); Photoshot p. 19 (EPA/ Rehan Khan); Rex Features p. 29 (Monkey Business Images); Shutterstock pp. 13 (© arindambanerjee), p 14 (© Susan DeLoach), p 21 (© Ammit).

Cover photograph of rescue workers searching through the smoking ruins of the CTV building in Christchurch reproduced with permission of Getty Images (Marty Melville/AFP).

Every effort has been made to contact copyright holders of material reproduced in this book. Any omissions will be rectified in subsequent printings if notice is given to the publisher.

We would like to thank Rachel Thompson for her invaluable help in the preparation of this book.

Disclaimer
All the internet addresses (URLs) given in this book were valid at the time of going to press. However, due to the dynamic nature of the internet, some addresses may have changed, or sites may have changed or ceased to exist since publication. While the author and publisher regret any inconvenience this may cause readers, no responsibility for any such changes can be accepted by either the author or the publisher.

Some words are shown in bold, **like this**. You can find out what they mean by looking in the glossary.

Contents

Disaster strikes!

It's a race against time! A **natural disaster** has struck somewhere in the world. **Earthquakes** and hurricanes are both kinds of natural disaster. People need help, and they need it quickly.

Did you know?
Earthquakes often make the ground shake and buildings collapse. These disaster **relief workers** were called into action when an earthquake hit Haiti in 2010.

Meet the relief team

When disaster strikes, relief teams have many jobs to do. Some **relief workers** search for **survivors**. Doctors and nurses care for injured people. Volunteers help to unblock roads and engineers make the roads safe.

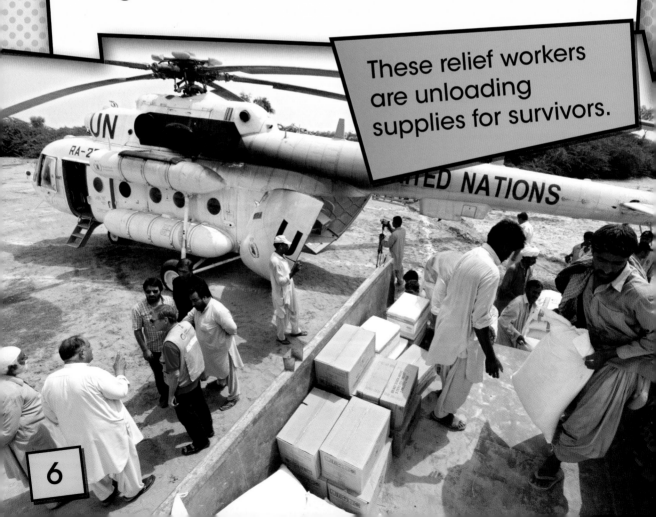

These relief workers are unloading supplies for survivors.

Helicopter pilots search the disaster area for people who need help.

First response

Rescuers have to reach the **disaster zone** quickly to save lives. When they arrive, the first job is to rescue people who may be trapped or injured. If **relief workers** find **survivors** quickly, they can save lives.

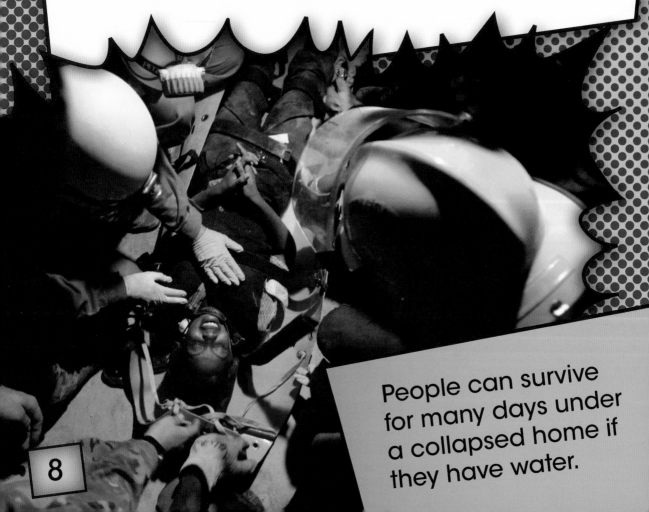

People can survive for many days under a collapsed home if they have water.

Keeping people alive

Disaster **survivors** need clean water and food as soon as possible. **Relief workers** may have to cross flooded land to reach them.

Did you know?
Drinking dirty water can cause diseases. Rescuers clean dirty water with **water treatment equipment** and special chemicals.

Treating the injured

After a disaster, many injured people cannot get to a hospital. Doctors and nurses sometimes work day and night in the open air to save people's lives.

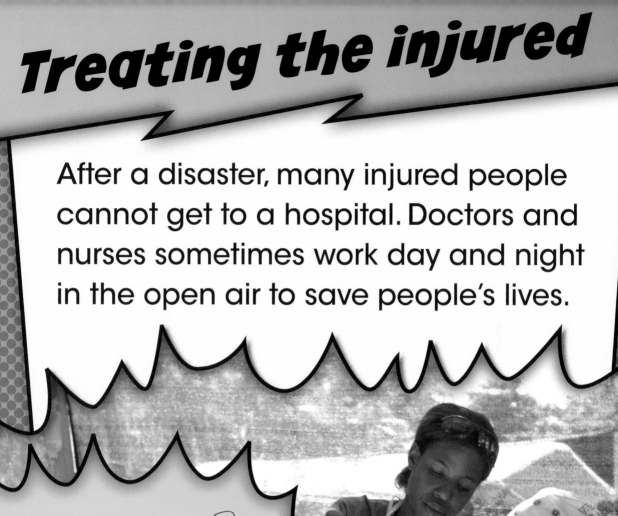

Did you know?
Many injuries treated after an **earthquake** are broken and crushed bones caused by collapsing buildings.

Tents and other temporary shelters are often built to protect people from the hot sun or cold nights.

What do rescuers need?

Disaster relief teams need lots of equipment, from helicopters to **tablets** that can clean water. Rescuers often use specially-trained dogs to sniff out injured people, using their strong sense of smell.

Did you know?

People's bodies give off heat. Rescuers sometimes use heat-sensing equipment to find people under the rubble.

15

Flood warning

When rivers or lakes overflow, **floods** can wash away roads and fill people's homes with muddy water. In deep water, boats are one way to rescue people trapped in buildings.

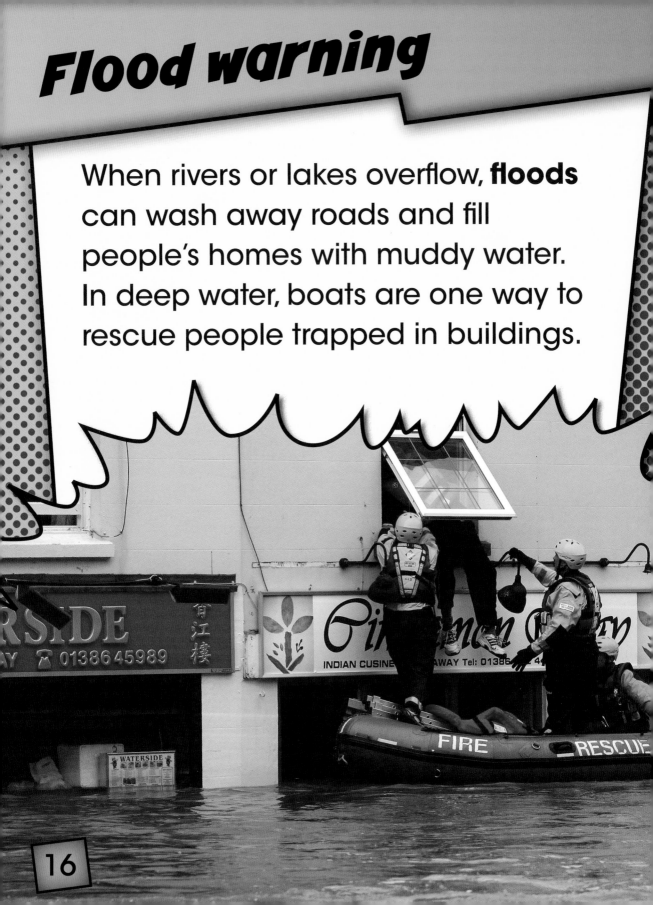

Did you know?
Heavy rains can cause violent **flash floods**. Queensland, Australia, was hit by flash flooding in 2011. Rescuers had to pull **survivors** from their cars or homes as they were carried away by the flood.

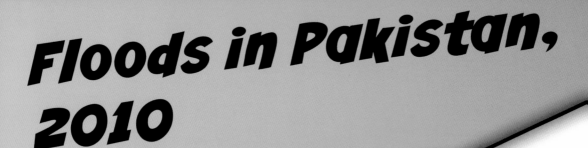

Floods in Pakistan, 2010

In 2010, **floods** in Pakistan covered an area the size of England. **Relief workers** used boats and helicopters to reach people in the flooded areas. They helped to provide shelter, water, food, and medical help.

Families who have lost their homes may move into large camps.

Volcano disaster

Volcanoes can **erupt**, or explode, throwing out hot rocks, ash, and **lava** from under the surface of the Earth. The lava, or hot liquid rock, burns anything in its path, including people's homes. Rescue workers have to wear masks and other protective clothing to keep safe.

Did you know?
When a volcano erupts, clouds of steaming hot gas can burn people in seconds.

Disasters in nature

Disasters can affect animals too. **Oil spills** are caused when oil leaks from huge tankers or oil drilling rigs into the sea and on to land. Animals can get covered in sticky oil.

Did you know?
In 2010, **relief workers** had to deal with a huge oil spill in the Gulf of Mexico. If the animals covered in oil were not cleaned, they would die.

Working in disaster relief

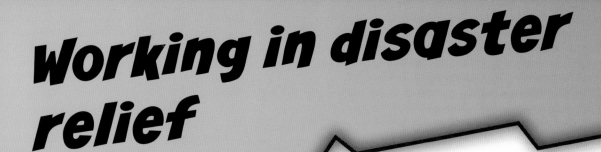

Many different people need to work together when disaster strikes. Doctors need to treat **survivors**. **Engineers** have to make sure buildings are safe. **Relief workers** must be tough enough to work under great pressure.

These rescue workers are cleaning up after a tsunami hit Japan in 2011.

Dangerous job

Disaster **relief workers** often put themselves in danger to help others. Diseases can spread quickly after a disaster. Even rescue workers can get caught up in **floods** and **hurricanes**.

Did you know?
Earthquakes are often followed by aftershocks. These can be as dangerous as the first earthquake. Buildings that have been weakened can still collapse.

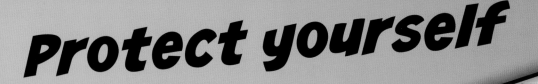

Protect yourself

Hopefully you will never be caught in a disaster. But you can be prepared with the following simple survival kit:

- a first aid kit
- clean drinking water
- food that won't go off
- a torch.

Storms that cause heavy snowfalls can often cause problems for people.

Did you know?
We can all help disaster relief by giving money or raising money for people who need help.

Glossary

disaster zone area affected by a disaster

earthquake violent shaking of the ground caused by movements of the Earth

engineer person trained to build and repair machinery and buildings

erupt explode, particularly used to describe hot ash and rock exploding out of a volcano

flash flood sudden and violent flood caused by very heavy rain

flood when a large amount of water flows over dry land

hurricane powerful storm with very high winds and heavy rain. Also called a typhoon or tropical storm.

lava hot liquid rock that comes out of a volcano

natural disaster disaster caused by forces of nature

oil spill disaster that happens when oil is released into the sea or on to land

relief worker person who works to help people affected by disasters

survivor person who is affected by a disaster but is still alive

tablet pill containing medicine

water treatment equipment things used to clean dirty water so it can be used for drinking

Find out more

Books

Earthquakes (Graphic Science), Katharine Krohn (Raintree Publishers, 2011)

Hurricane Hunters and Tornado Chasers (Graphic Careers), Gary Jeffrey (Franklin Watts, 2010)

Natural Disasters, Andrew Langley (Kingfisher, 2008)

Websites

earthquake.usgs.gov/learn/kids/
Visit this site to find out all about earthquakes, what causes them, and the damage they can do.

www.fema.gov/kids/dizarea.htm
This website looks at lots of different types of natural disaster.

www.oxfam.org.uk/coolplanet/kidsweb/world/index.htm
This webpage is part of the charity Oxfam's Cool Planet site. It has links to Oxfam's activities around the world, including disaster relief.

Index